Oxford CONNECTIONS

Victorian Children

Lynn Huggins-Cooper

Series editor Sue Palmer

OXFORD
UNIVERSITY PRESS

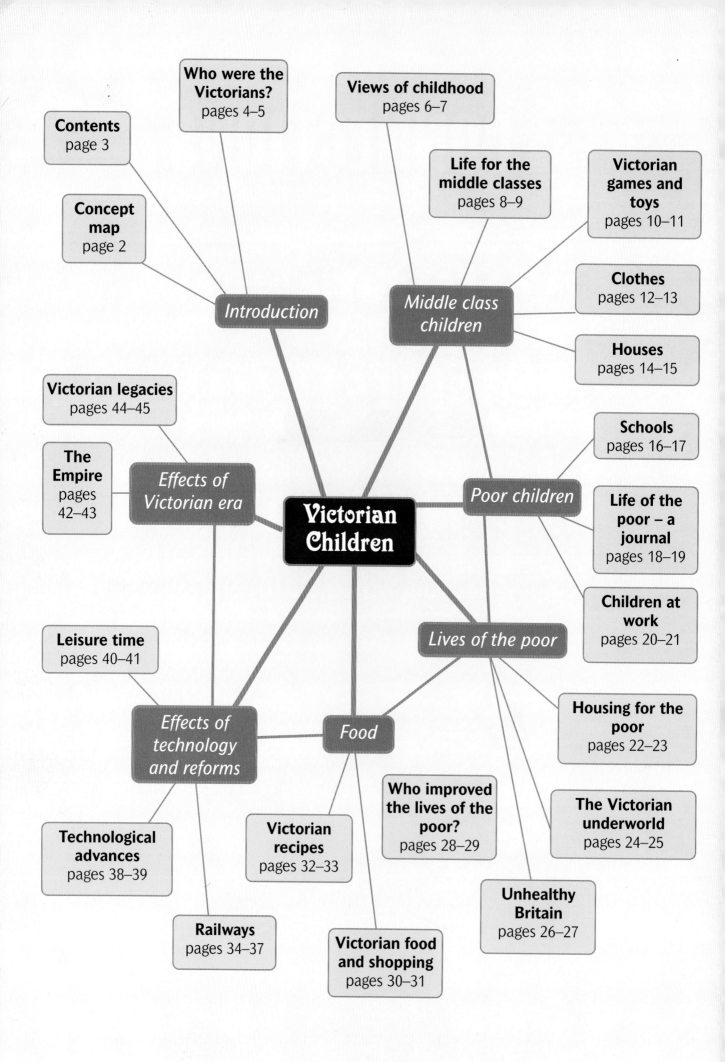

Contents
page 3

Concept map
page 2

Who were the Victorians?
pages 4–5

Views of childhood
pages 6–7

Life for the middle classes
pages 8–9

Victorian games and toys
pages 10–11

Clothes
pages 12–13

Houses
pages 14–15

Introduction

Middle class children

Victorian Children

Victorian legacies
pages 44–45

The Empire
pages 42–43

Effects of Victorian era

Poor children

Schools
pages 16–17

Life of the poor – a journal
pages 18–19

Children at work
pages 20–21

Lives of the poor

Housing for the poor
pages 22–23

Leisure time
pages 40–41

Effects of technology and reforms

Food

Who improved the lives of the poor?
pages 28–29

The Victorian underworld
pages 24–25

Technological advances
pages 38–39

Victorian recipes
pages 32–33

Unhealthy Britain
pages 26–27

Railways
pages 34–37

Victorian food and shopping
pages 30–31

Contents

This book provides a lot of information about people's different ways of life in Victorian times. It describes how poor people lived and ways in which people tried to improve their lives. I particularly enjoyed reading about Victorian children and found it interesting to compare Victorian schools with schools of today.

Dr Penelope Harnett
Principal Lecturer in Education,
University of the West of
England, Bristol

Who were the Victorians?

Portrait of Queen Victoria painted in 1886

Queen Victoria came to the throne in 1837. She was only 18 years old. She reigned for over 63 years – longer than any other British king or queen.

The growing empire

During Queen Victoria's reign, Britain became the most powerful nation in the world. Britain's **empire** grew to an enormous size. It stretched from Canada to New Zealand, and covered an amazing fifth of the world. Britain became very rich through the goods that poured in from all the countries in the empire. Wealth also increased through the growth of industry.

A divided society

This 'growth of **industry**' and the many technological changes helped throughout the era to create a society of three groups of people: the **upper class**, the **middle class** and the **working class**. The working class tended to work long hours in dirty

1837 — Victoria became Queen, aged 18

1847 — Law passed banning women and children under 18 from working more than 10 hours a day in factories

1848 — Public Health Act allowed towns to set up companies to build sewers and drains

1851 — The Great Exhibition

1852 — All main railway routes completed

1866 — First transatlantic telegraph cable

4

and dangerous jobs to create wealth for the upper and middle classes. Even very young children had to work to help their families survive. The middle classes increased as many more people owned businesses, or worked as managers or professionals. Middle class fathers earned enough money to buy a home, and their wives and children did not have to work. They were even able to employ servants.

Wages differed enormously. Poor children working in factories might earn £10 for a year's labour. An engineer could earn about £110 per year and a professional man, such as a senior civil servant, might earn around £700.

An age of reforms

A series of **Reform Acts** introduced during the Victorian era attempted to improve the lives of the poor, stopping very young children from working in mines and factories. Free schooling was introduced for everyone. Health reforms also attempted to make life better, by providing cleaner water, **sewers** and hospitals for even the poorest people.

The growth of technology

The Victorian era could be called 'The Age of Invention'. The invention of much of the technology we take for granted in the modern world – such as telephones and typewriters – took place at this time. Transport developed quickly. By 1852 all the main railway routes in Britain had been built.

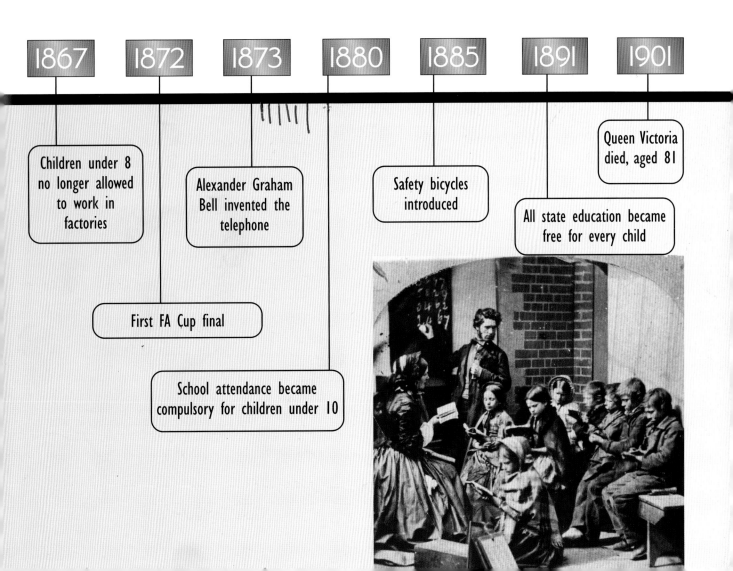

| 1867 | 1872 | 1873 | 1880 | 1885 | 1891 | 1901 |

Children under 8 no longer allowed to work in factories

Alexander Graham Bell invented the telephone

Safety bicycles introduced

Queen Victoria died, aged 81

All state education became free for every child

First FA Cup final

School attendance became compulsory for children under 10

Views of childhood

It is said that in the Victorian era the way in which society looked at its children changed drastically.

In the **middle class** Victorian family, children were seen as innocent. Childhood was a special time in which the young should be shaped and protected by their parents. Poor children, however, had a very different experience. Their families did not love them any less, but their children had to work because they needed the wages their children could earn.

For the middle class family, childhood was not just seen as a time for training for adulthood, but also a time for play. On the other hand, poor children were employed in many dangerous and unpleasant places such as textile factories and mines. Therefore, they did not have time to play.

The same middle class people, who saw their own children as needing protection, were often guilty of making their money from child labour – the children of the poor. As a result, a poor child had a childhood of hard work, pain and hunger.

Children's books first became popular in the Victorian period. They described childhood as a special time of play and exploration as well as a time to learn how to behave. They also told of the terrible consequences that bad behaviour brought! These books, however, were written by middle class people for middle class children. Many poor children were unable to read because they did not go to school and learn.

So it is fair to say that childhood did change, but only for those children of middle class families.

ON THE WALL TOP.

So high—so high on the wall we run,
The nearer the sky—why, the nearer the sun.
If you give me one penny, I'll give you two,
For that's the way good neighbours do.

Kate Greenaway was a well-known Victorian author and illustrator who wrote many books for children.

Illustration entitled 'Baby Brother' from a Victorian children's book

Photograph taken in about 1860 of poor children in London

Childhood is a golden time. I like to surround my children with beautiful toys, and books like Kate Greenaway's, so they can have a magical childhood.

I love my oldest child as much as any other mother would. But she has to work to help us survive. She has little time to play, and even rest. I hate her having to work but what else can I do?

Children are clean slates on which we write instructions on **morals**, right and wrong, and the correct way to behave. 'Spare the rod, and spoil the child' is the motto we live by.

I wish my children could have a better life. Hunger gnaws at their bellies and they spend their days in the dark of the factory. But they need to work – it's that or the **workhouse** for us.

7

Life for the middle classes

Maria, aged 9

William, aged 6

Milly the maid

Nanny

Mama

Papa

6 o'clock: Awake in nursery – Milly lights fire

8 o'clock: Breakfast

I'm going to the surgery.

9 o'clock: Time to play

10 o'clock: Reading with Nanny

11 o'clock: Walk to market

I want to buy some liquorice.

I want to buy some little cups and saucers.

12 o'clock: Luncheon

2 o'clock: Mother has guests

Come quietly to the nursery for lessons.

3 o'clock: High tea

4 o'clock: Walk

6 o'clock: Preparing for bed

6.30: Going to father's study

Now you've said your prayers, you can have a small biscuit.

Biscuits

7 o'clock: Bedtime

Victorian games and toys

In Victorian times, many popular toys were made from cheaply produced tin as well as wood. Tumbling acrobats, such as the one shown opposite, would be quite cheap, and could be enjoyed by all but the poorest children. The poorest often had no toys, or only toys made from materials found as rubbish, such as dolls made from rags.

The Bethnal Green Museum of Childhood in London has many examples of Victorian toys such as the tumbling acrobat, toy soldiers, dolls and their houses, teddies and zoetropes (magical boxes that, when spun, seem to show a film).

How to make a Victorian flicker book

You will need:

- paper to draw your flicker pictures
- felt-tipped pens or coloured pencils
- scissors
- stapler

A filoscope is like a flicker book but has a lever to turn the pages.

Method:

1 Draw 10 equal-sized boxes with a pencil and ruler on paper.

2 Draw a picture in each box to create a sequence. A good sequence would be a person kicking a ball.

3 Colour in the pictures. Keep the colours the same from picture to picture.

4 Cut out all of the boxes to make pages.

5 Stack the pages, face up, in order.

6 Staple the pages together with one staple at the very top.

7 Hold at the top and flip the pages from back to front. Watch your picture move!

How to make your own Victorian tumbling clown

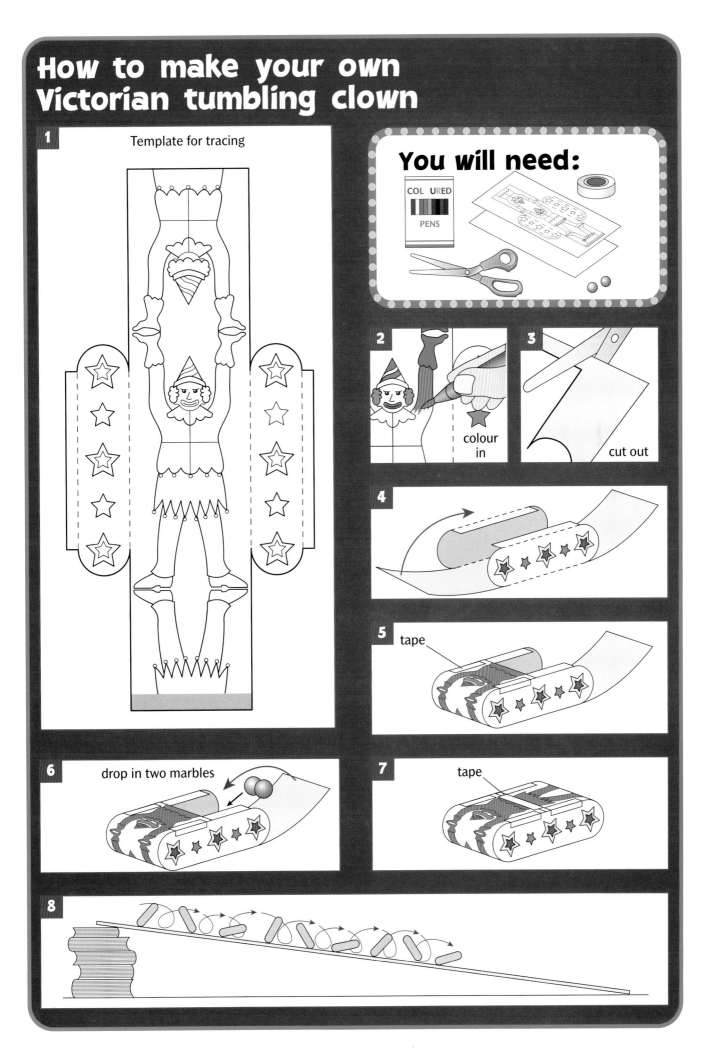

1 Template for tracing

You will need:

COL URED PENS

2 colour in

3 cut out

4

5 tape

6 drop in two marbles

7 tape

8

Clothes

What did Victorian children wear?

Children without rich parents would be working, often when still very young. They wore smaller versions of the clothes adults wore, or even adult clothes cut down and rolled up to make them fit. In poor families, children often wore 'hand me downs' – clothes worn by the eldest child and then passed down to younger children.

Children from richer families dressed rather differently from poorer children. For girls and for boys, clothes were heavy and impractical. They must have made any sort of free or active play very difficult. They were also hard to keep clean and tidy. In **middle class** and rich families, servants would wash and iron the frilly clothes and keep them repaired.

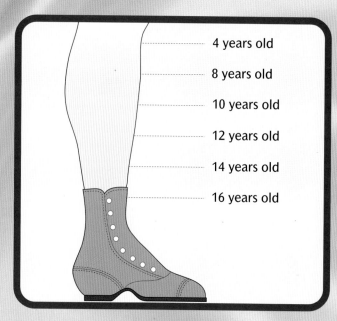

4 years old
8 years old
10 years old
12 years old
14 years old
16 years old

There were clear rules on how long skirts had to be. It was seen as improper to show your ankles after the age of 16.

Adults' clothes were very **modest**, covering the body completely.

It's a boy! Or is it a girl?

Wealthy Victorian boys wore dresses when they were young. In some photographs, it is difficult to tell whether a child is a boy or a girl – the boys also had long hair, often prettily curled. Boys would usually have their hair cut by the age of eight. By the 1880s, this was becoming the accepted age to leave home for boarding school.

The age at which boys were 'breeched' – allowed to wear knee breeches – is uncertain, but paintings and photographs of the day give us clues. It probably happened at about four to five years of age.

Sailor style

'Sailor suits' were very popular, for boys and girls. Queen Victoria's decision to dress the Prince of Wales and his brothers in sailor suits first introduced the style to the public. The style was widely worn by boys during the 1870s.

A wealthy boy in a sailor suit

'Little Lord Fauntleroy' suits had elaborate lace collars.

Some mothers in the late-19th century dressed their sons in 'Little Lord Fauntleroy' suits with lace collars. This fashion started because of the children's book *Little Lord Fauntleroy* by Frances Hodgson Burnett.

Extracts from *Little Lord Fauntleroy*, describing the remarkably good-looking and well-behaved boy.

Though he was born in so quiet and cheap a little home, it seemed as if there never had been a more fortunate baby. In the first place, he was always well, and so he never gave any one trouble; in the second place, he had so sweet a temper and ways so charming that he was a pleasure to every one; and in the third place, he was so beautiful to look at that he was quite a picture. Instead of being a bald-headed baby, he started in life with a quantity of soft, fine, gold-colored hair, which curled up at the ends, and went into loose rings by the time he was six months old; he had big brown eyes and long eyelashes and a darling little face; he had so strong a back and such splendid sturdy legs, that at nine months he learned suddenly to walk; his manners were so good, for a baby, that it was delightful to make his acquaintance.

When he was old enough to walk out with his nurse, dragging a small wagon and wearing a short white kilt skirt, and a big white hat set back on his curly yellow hair, he was so handsome and strong and rosy that he attracted every one's attention, and his nurse would come home and tell his mamma stories of the ladies who had stopped their carriages to look at and speak to him, and of how pleased they were when he talked to them in his cheerful little way, as if he had known them always.

Houses

In Victorian times, homes varied from the large detached houses of the wealthy to the overcrowded tenements of the poor. **Middle class** houses, like the one shown here, had many ornate rooms with heavy carved wood furniture, velvet and brocade fabrics, and lots of ornaments. Servants worked unseen in the scullery and kitchen. Maids cleaned the house, and a cook prepared the meals. Many poorer young people went 'into service' (became servants) and worked very hard, for long hours.

Bathroom

In early Victorian times, middle class houses had bathrooms with wooden washstands, a bowl and pitcher, and a tin bath. By the 1870s, indoor plumbing and hot water made bathing a pleasure. Large, colourful sinks and enamelled baths on ball-and-claw or scroll feet appeared, as did indoor toilets.

Decoration

Before Victorian times almost everything used to make a house had to be made by hand – even the nails! As technology developed, many of these items were made with machines instead. This made them more easily available, and cheaper. Factories produced banisters, cornices and other such decorative items, which the middle classes could afford to buy.

Fancy brass or iron bedsteads

Drawing room – for receiving guests and entertaining

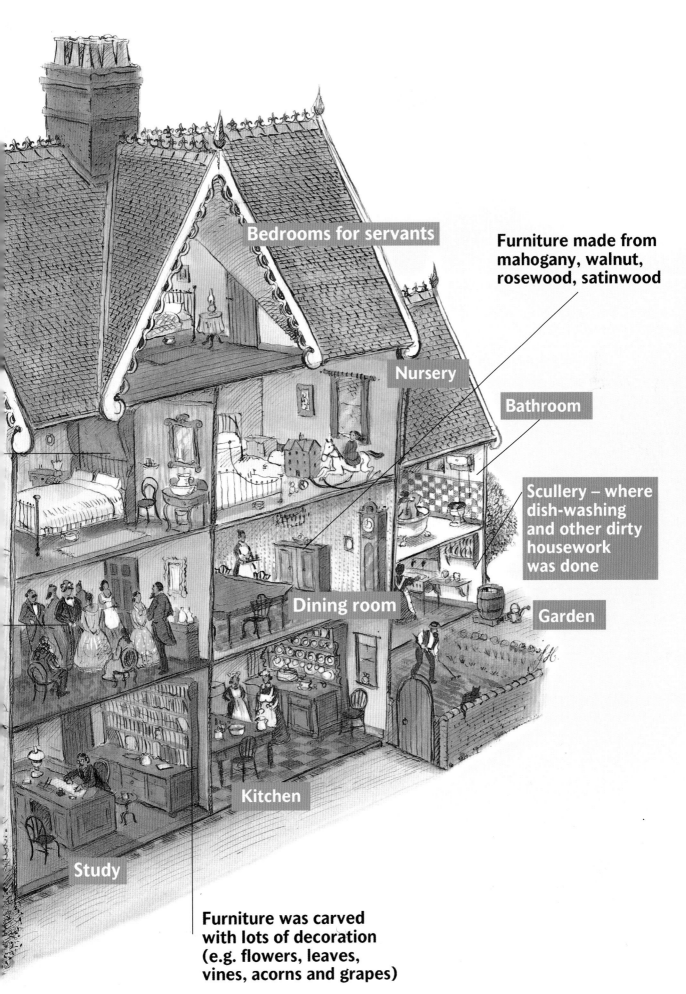

Bedrooms for servants

Furniture made from mahogany, walnut, rosewood, satinwood

Nursery

Bathroom

Scullery – where dish-washing and other dirty housework was done

Dining room

Garden

Kitchen

Study

Furniture was carved with lots of decoration (e.g. flowers, leaves, vines, acorns and grapes)

Schools

In early Victorian times, most children did not go to school as many of them had to work. Poorer children could attend Sunday school, provided by churches, but the staff were often untrained and there was little equipment. There were some dame schools, which were run by elderly women. Other schools for orphans and very poor children (called 'ragged' schools) were organized by churches and charities.

In later Victorian times, all children had to go to school until they were 13, but it was free of charge. This was the beginning of a national system of schools, with education for everyone regardless of whether they were rich or poor. As a result, many new schools were created.

Classrooms were often crowded. Before 1850, a single teacher might have had to instruct a class of over a hundred children.

Teachers

Teachers were very strict (see Discipline) and were not well paid. They were often helped by 'pupil teachers'. These were usually bright, but poor pupils, who were training to be teachers. Classes were often huge and all the pupils had to do the same thing at the same time.

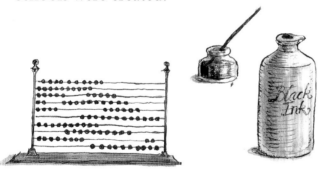

Children of wealthy families

The children of wealthy families had nannies, and then a governess or tutor to teach them at home. Later, boys would be sent away to boarding school, with girls staying at home to learn to fulfil their future roles as wives by learning 'social graces' such as playing the piano and embroidery.

Few schools had a well-equipped gym like this.

Lessons

Children learned to write on slates, scratching letters on them with sharpened pieces of slate. Paper was very expensive. Older children learned to write with a pen and ink by writing in **copybooks**. The ink was kept in clay inkwells.

Victorian clay inkwell

They copied work from the blackboard or from books. Lessons concentrated on the 'Three Rs': Reading', 'wRiting' and 'aRithmetic'. They also spent large periods of time chanting things to 'learn' them. It was not an exciting way to learn!

Children had to pass exams in maths, reading and writing before they could move up to the next class or 'standard'. This would be very embarrassing for children who found learning hard – they would be left behind with the little ones as their friends moved on.

	Monday	Tuesday	Wednesday	Thursday	Friday
Ten to nine	Entrance drill	Entrance drill	Entrance drill	Entrance drill	Entrance drill
Nine o'clock	Prayers	Prayers	Prayers	Prayers	Prayers
Ten minutes after nine	Scripture	Scripture	Scripture	Scripture	Scripture
Ten o'clock	Arithmetic	Arithmetic	Arithmetic	Arithmetic	Arithmetic
Eleven o'clock	Recreation	Recreation	Recreation	Recreation	Recreation
Ten minutes after eleven	Reading	Dictation	Drill	Dictation	Spelling
One o'clock	Prayers	Prayers	Prayers	Prayers	Prayers
Ten minutes after one	Drill	Spelling	Reading	Dictation and writing	Dictation and writing
Two o'clock	Geography	Singing	Object lesson	Needlework/ woodwork	Drill
Three o'clock	Spelling	Reading	Writing	Reading	Writing

A typical school timetable

Discipline

Victorian teachers used a cane or strap to punish their pupils. Schools had 'punishment books' to record the pupils' behaviour and the punishments given.

Pupils could be beaten for 'rude conduct', answering back, missing Sunday prayers, leaving the playground without permission, making blots and smudges in their copybooks, sulkiness, throwing ink pellets and being late. Pupils were also punished by being made to stand on a stool at the back of the class, wearing an armband with 'DUNCE' (a word that means stupid) written on it, and a tall pointed hat with a 'D' on the front.

1910	Department.	School.			Principal Teacher
No. Name		Offence	Date of Offence	Punishment Awarded	Date of Punishment
1 Geo Edwards		taking sweets from small boy	Jan 19	2 strokes	Jan 19
2 Albert Breakspear			"	"	"
3 Wyn Howse		sent out due to giving trouble	" 21		Jan 21
4 Harry Cook		Late through playing marbles	Feb 7	1 "	Feb 7
5 Dorothy James		Troublesome in class and refusing to come out	Feb 8	2 "	Feb 8
6 Victor Woodage		playing in Mr Smith's farmyard during dinnertime	Apr 13	1 "	Apr 13
7 Ernest Smith			"	1 "	"
8 George Fisher			"	1 "	"
9 Victor Woodage		playing in class when master absent from room	Apr 14	1 "	Apr 14
10 Albert Breakspear			"	1 "	
11 Herbert Hunt		throwing across class	May 5	2 "	May 5
12 Ernest Smith		playing in Mr Smith's barn during dinnertime	July 8	2 "	July 8
13 George Fisher			"	2 "	
14 Stanley Pound			"	2 "	
15 John Dowling		Stealing boy's dinner	July 25	6 on posterior	July 25

Excerpt from a punishment book, 1890

Dunce's cap

17

Life of the poor - a journal

Got up at 5 o'clock and set off for Bryant and May's match factory. I started work at half-past 5 sharp because it's summer (I start at 8 in winter). If a girl is late she is shut out for half the day, and loses pay – so I daren't be late! I'm what they call a piece-worker. I got 3 shillings last week. We do all right.

My sister Clarrie got me the job. She works at the factory, and earns good money, as much as 8 shillings or 9 shillings a week. Out of our earnings we pay 2 shillings for the rent of our one room.

At 9 o'clock I had my half-an-hour break for breakfast and ate a slice of bread, with a bottle of cold tea. By breakfast my feet were aching. I have to stand on my feet all day long, and they don't half swell!

At 11 o'clock we heard terrible squealing and banging. Dora's fingers had got caught in the machine and she'd only just pulled them free in time. She was fined a shilling for letting the web twist round a machine to save her fingers from being cut. The foreman said, "Take care of the machine, never mind your fingers." Girls get hurt all the time.

At half-past 1, a woman called Mrs Besant came round during our lunch break to talk to some of the girls. She says the way we work is a disgrace and she'll help us. I do hope so. But I don't want to lose my job. The **Workhouse** scares me even more than the **phossy jaw!**

My friend Jenny got fined this afternoon. Her feet were dirty, and the ground under the benches was mucky. When the foreman came round inspecting our work at 3 o'clock, she got fined threepence. Her mam will go spare. Last week, Jenny's sister Kate got fined a whole shilling! She put 'burnts' (matches that have caught fire during the work) on the bench.

At 4 o'clock, just as he was finishing his rounds, the foreman nearly caught me talking. I was that relieved to see his back disappearing. You get fined for talking, too. He gave me a hard stare but I put my best 'innocent' face on. Sometimes you get clouted off the foreman, so it's best to keep quiet.

We use phosphorous to make the matches. We get called 'canaries' sometimes because our skin goes yellow. Some of the girls even have trouble with their hair that falls out in clumps. It's terrible. When I passed by Bella's table at half-past 5, while I was tidying up, she showed me a handful of her hair that had dropped out during the day. But what I'm scared of is the phossy jaw. One of the old girls got it. They were talking about her when we were getting our coats on at 6 o'clock, ready to go home. The whole side of her face turned green and then black, and they said she had horrible-smelling pus coming out of her jaw.

Once a month we go out to a real slap up meal where you get coffee, and bread and butter, jam, and marmalade. By half-past 6 I was sitting down in the warm, my mouth crammed with food. My stomach had been grumbling for it all day.

It's 8 o'clock now and I'm curled up for the night next to Clarrie. Early start again tomorrow.

Did you know?

Twelve pennies (d.) equalled a shilling (s.); twenty shillings (s.) made a pound (£).

Sample prices in 1840
1 4lb-loaf cost 3d.
1 pint of beer cost 2d.
1 pint of milk cost 1d.
1 stamp to send a letter anywhere in Britain cost 1d.

Children at work

The following interviews are based on real interviews with doctors about the health of children working in factories. They are both based on eyewitness accounts of the conditions children endured. They give very different viewpoints. As historians it is important that we think about reasons WHY people gave the opinions they did when we read original documents and evidence.

Which of these pictures of cotton factories is the most reliable source of information – the drawing or the photograph?

Charles Benton was interviewed by a House of Commons Committee.

Question: **Who asked you to carry out the surveys?**

Answer: The Chairman of the Committee of cotton spinners. They chose the seven factories in Manchester I visited.

Question: **What were your findings?**

Answer: Ventilation was good, and the children and adults working in the factories enjoyed good health.

Question: **Did the children growing up in the factories appear to be less healthy than those in other occupations?**

Answer: No. I have not found them worse-looking.

Question: **Are you saying that terrible conditions – such as standing for 15-hour days in high temperatures – does not affect their health?**

Answer: I can't answer that question.

Question: **Are injuries common in the factories?**

Answer: I am not aware of any injuries.

Dr William Henry was interviewed by a House of Lords Committee

Question: **How many factories did you visit?**

Answer: I visited three factories in Preston and Manchester but could not stay more than 10 minutes in the dusty atmosphere of each without gasping for breath. How can workers – even children – endure up to 15 hours of this?

Question: **How does the health of children working in cotton factories compare to children elsewhere?**

Answer: It is much worse. The factories are nurseries of disease and vice – not at all suitable for children! Children are injured with hands and arms caught in machinery and skin stripped to the bone. Fingers are regularly lost. I visited a school recently where 106 children worked in the factories – 47 of these children had been injured! They are beaten and become deformed until they are unable to run and play.

These doctors held very different views about the effects that working in factories had on the health of children. The argument raged as reformers tried to stop children from working in dangerous conditions – not just in mills and factories, but in mines and as chimney sweeps too.

Can you think of a reason why some doctors, like Charles Benton, would support the use of child labour? Think about the fact that some doctors' wages were paid by factory owners.

"When I first went to the mill we worked from six in the morning till seven in the evening. After a time we began at five in the morning, and worked till ten at night. We were beaten, and constantly tired.

I had stuff to rub on my knees; and I used to rub my joints for a quarter of an hour, and sometimes an hour or two.

Because of the hard work, I have an iron on my leg; my knee is contracted. The surgeons in the Infirmary told me my deformity was caused by standing. The marrow is dried out of the bone, so that there is no natural strength in it. Before I worked in the mill I could run and play. Not now."

Based on a real interview with a young mill worker in 1832

Housing for the poor

All across Victorian Britain, poor people were living in **slums** – terrible housing with dreadful conditions in cities, towns and villages. They did not own their homes but had to pay rent.

Some of the worst were the overcrowded **tenements** in cities such as Glasgow. These tenements were like blocks of flats where many poor families lived together in dirty conditions.

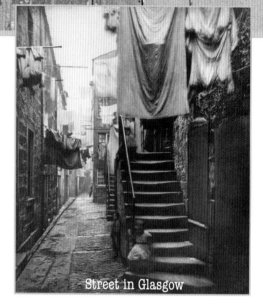
Street in Glasgow

Slums in London

The poor in the countryside often lived in cottages owned by the local landowners who they worked for. These homes often had dirt floors and no running water.

The poor in the industrial north of England lived in 'back-to-back' housing (sets of houses joined together with one or two rooms upstairs and down). It was dark, dirty and overcrowded, often in areas where soot and dust from factories filled the sky.

WORKHOUSES

- Large housing, like a prison, for the poorest families
- Families split up
- Inmates chopped wood, broke stones for road building
- Gruel to eat (thin porridge)

Books about life for the Victorian poor:
Dickens – *Oliver Twist*; Leon Garfield – *Smith*

An engraving showing overcrowded housing conditions

OVERCROWDING

- Large families – six or seven children per family
- Entire families crammed into single rooms
- Many homes were also workshops (families took in dressmaking or laundry, or made matchboxes)

HOUSING FOR THE POOR

Cartoon reminding people that cholera spreads through bad food

DIRT AND DISEASE

- Filthy conditions – stinking waste everywhere
- **Sewage** flowed in the streets in 'open **sewers**'
- Sewage ran into rivers – **contaminated** drinking water
- Water from a shared pump in the street – often only one standpipe turned on for 20 minutes a day
- Dirty water and crowded conditions led to spread of diseases
- Filth and pollution led to pests – fleas, lice, bed bugs, rats

The Victorian underworld

The Victorian underworld was made up of criminals such as shoplifters, highway robbers, **pickpockets** and **cutpurses**. The Victorian era was a time of great wealth – and great poverty. **Social reformers** said that it was perhaps this extreme poverty that made people turn to crime.

Henry Mayhew

Henry Mayhew wrote a series of books called *London Labour and the London Poor*. He was particularly interested in the lives of people in 'the underworld' and in the poor, who he called the '**underclasses**'.

An engraving from Mayhew's *Prisons of London*

In some prisons, inmates were made to walk on the spot all day, to turn a treadmill round and round.

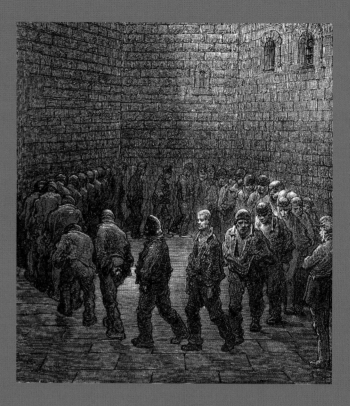

Punishments

Punishments for crime were fierce. They included 'hard labour' – being sent to prison to break rocks, move soil for building works and clear **sewers**. The idea was that hard work would 'reform' the prisoners – and make them sorry for what they had done.

Execution

Many prisoners got the death sentence. People were hanged in a gruesome public spectacle. The Victorians believed that this would put other people off committing crimes.

The prison population

The prison population was so huge that 'hulks' (rotting old ships that were permanently moored) also served as prisons. Many of the prisoners died of disease, as well as the hard work and lack of decent food. At the start of Victoria's

Public executions ended in 1868 – too many people in the viewing crowds were robbed and murdered!

reign, 3625 prisoners were held in hulks.

By 1857, the prisoners held in this way had all been transported (shipped to Australia). The voyage was long and hard, and many prisoners died in the poor conditions. Once they got to Australia, they worked in harsh conditions and many more died.

Child crime

The Victorians were shocked that children committed crimes, because children were supposed to be innocent. Even before Victoria came to the throne, Parliament had set up a 'Committee for Investigating the Alarming Increase in Juvenile Crime in the Metropolis' (London). Social reformers, such as Mary Carpenter, pointed out that children from extremely poor or criminal families were far more likely to commit crimes, and she said that perhaps they had not had the chance to learn right from wrong. She argued that children, when put into prison with adults,

Books such as Dickens' *Oliver Twist*, published in 1837, increased the panic about gangs of pickpockets and robbers. This engraving shows the Artful Dodger teaching Oliver Twist how to pickpocket from the rich.

merely learned how to commit even more crimes.

The Juvenile Offences Act of 1847 said that young people under 14 should be tried in a special court, not an adult court. In 1854, the first Reformatory Schools were created. Children were sent to these 'schools' for years, with the idea that they would be taken away from 'bad influences'. The children were treated harshly, with frequent whippings and only bread and water to eat and drink.

Unhealthy Britain

In early Victorian Britain, thousands of people died every year from illness and disease. The main causes were a lack of proper **sewage** systems and clean water supplies. Sewage was thrown into rivers. Drinking water was taken from the same rivers, so diseases such as **cholera** were easily spread.

While infectious diseases spread particularly quickly amongst the poor because of their overcrowded housing, rich families were affected as well. Even Prince Albert, Queen Victoria's husband, died of typhoid (a disease that spread in the same way as cholera). However, the spread of disease amongst the rich was lessened by the fact that their family homes were larger – a sick person could be kept away from other members of the household and away from the preparation of food.

As a result of the lack of a proper sewage system in London the 'Great Stink' happened. In 1858, the River Thames had become so polluted and smelly that people refused to use the river-steamers and would walk miles to avoid crossing the city bridges. Parliament could carry on its business only by hanging disinfectant-soaked cloths over the windows. The curtains were soaked in chloride of lime. Parliament quickly passed a law in just 18 days to provide money to build large new **sewers** for London.

It was evident that something had to be done about the sewage systems in all towns and cities and when the cause of cholera had been proven, the race was on to provide clean drinking water and new sewers in all new towns.

In 1857, 250 tonnes of raw sewage washed into the River Thames every day. People drank the water, and so the river was a source of disease and death.

Pollution from factories and the coal burned in fires led to lung diseases. Rotting food often made poor people sick. Lead in water pipes was slowly poisoning people, rich as well as poor.

Food was often kept in unhygienic conditions.

Doctors and disease

Little was known about the causes of disease, and going to a doctor – if you could afford to – could make you feel worse or even kill you. Doctors did not know how diseases spread. They believed that a **miasma** was the cause because many epidemics happened during the summer time when rotting rubbish left in the streets gave off a strong smell. In fact, doctors themselves spread diseases because they did not **sterilize** their instruments, use **antiseptics**, or even wash their hands before treating the next patient.

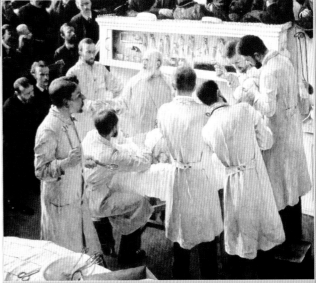
Operations were sometimes performed in front of an audience.

The improvers

While they were nurses in the Crimean War, Mary Seacole and Florence Nightingale saw that keeping things clean meant that fewer people died. Scientists such as Joseph Lister also improved conditions in hospitals by using antiseptics to kill germs.

The Victorian Times, 16th February 1854 – Letter to the Editor

Dear Sir

I am writing to inform those readers who are opposed to the programme of public spending on **sanitation** of the terrible health problems to be found in the middle of our city of London. I am writing to insist that they support the programme so that proper drains and clean water systems are provided.

I went to visit the Narrow Street area where a terrible outbreak of cholera had occurred. It is an area where the sewers are decaying and the **cesspits** are undrained. I have for some time believed that water full of germs spreads cholera from person to person. Here, cholera came from a single source of polluted water – the public water pump. I took a sample of the fetid water from the pump and looked at it under the microscope. It contained tiny white floating specks – the infection! I immediately went to the Board of Guardians of St John's Parish. I urged them to remove the pump handle to stop people from obtaining the infected water. They agreed and the spread of cholera dramatically dropped but not before 616 people had died.

Now that we know how cholera is spread, it is our duty to provide proper drains and an organized water system to banish the scourge of cholera from our streets forever.

Yours truly

Dr Snow
London

This letter is based on a real report from 1854 by Dr Snow, a medical doctor in London.

Who improved the lives of the poor?

Anthony Ashley Cooper, Earl of Shaftesbury (born 1801)

- Worked at improving living and working conditions
- 1847 introduced 10 Hour Act (limited working day of women and children)
- 1874 introduced Factory Act (illegal for under-14s to have full-time jobs)
- Died 1885

Edwin Chadwick (born 1800)

- Published report blaming slum conditions and dirty water/**sewage** problems for diseases
- Called for new sewage and water systems to be built
- Died 1890
- By 1900 towns had mains drainage and water systems

Henry Mayhew (born 1812)

- 1850s wrote *London Labour and the London Poor* (told people about conditions of the poor)
- Died 1887

William Booth (born 1829)

William Booth was born in Nottingham in 1829. At the age of 15 he became a Christian, and led meetings as a preacher. He believed strongly in social reforms to ease the suffering of the poor.

In 1852, William met Catherine Mumford who shared William's passion for justice. The couple were married on 16 June 1855.

Ten years later William and Catherine Booth opened the Whitechapel Christian Mission in

Annie Besant (born 1847)

1847 Born Clapham, London

1867 Married Frank Besant, clergyman

1873 Annie's irreligious views lead to separation

1870s Worked on weekly *National Reformer* (preached 'free thought', social and political reforms)

Editor of *The Link: A Journal for the Servants of Man*, a newspaper that told people about conditions of the poor

Helped Bryant & May workers form match-girls' union; helped organize 3-week strike (Bryant & May forced to agree to some changes)

1890s Became supporter of Theosophy (religious movement based on Hindu ideas)

1911 Main speaker at important **suffragette** rally

1916 While living in India joined struggle for **home rule**

1933 Died in India

Elizabeth Garrett Anderson (born 1836)

- First woman to qualify as a doctor
- Set up hospital for poor women and children in London
- Died 1917

Dr Barnado (born 1845)

- Opened homes for orphaned children in London from 1867 onwards
- By his death (1905) had opened 90 homes (charity still helps young people today)

London's East End, to offer food and shelter to the poor. They formed the Salvation Army in 1878; its aim was to bring food, shelter and religious instruction to the poor.

In 1891, the Salvation Army opened its own match-factory in Old Ford, East London. It used red phosphorous to make matches, which carried no risk to workers of '**phossy jaw**'. The factory paid workers twice the rate given at Bryant and May. (In 1901 Bryant and May stopped using dangerous yellow phosphorous themselves.)

William Booth organized tours of his factory for MPs and journalists. He also took them to homes of 'sweated workers' who worked 11 and 12 hours a day for companies like Bryant and May.

When William Booth died in 1912, his eldest son, William Bramwell Booth, became the leader of the Salvation Army.

In Victorian times, people shopped in local markets and stores every day for food. The arrival of the railways brought more fresh food to the inner cities. Most food was produced within Britain and was seasonal because there were no methods of keeping food fresh while transporting it from other countries. However, in the home, a variety of ways of preserving food were used, such as smoking and bottling in syrup. Salt, sugar or vinegar were used in salting, making jam and pickling. Tinned food was sold but it was often expensive and so not very widespread, although brand names such as Crosse and Blackwell and Heinz were established before the end of the century.

Mrs Beeton's recipes were so popular, they were republished many times. This edition is dated 1890.

Some foods were preserved in bottles with syrup or in brine (salt water). The first tinned foods also appeared in Victorian times.

In **upper-** and **middle-class** households, the servants would shop for the family, although tradesmen also visited houses to sell food directly to the housekeeper. One of the dilemmas facing the newer middle class wives was how to manage their households. *Mrs Beeton's Book of Household Management*, published in 1861, was written for this growing group of middle class women. It describes the role of the mistress of the house, comparing her to an army commander.

"What moved me ... was the discomfort and suffering which I had seen brought upon men and women by household mismanagement. I have always thought that there is no more fruitful source of family discontent than a housewife's badly cooked dinners and untidy ways. Men are now so well served out of doors – at their clubs, well-ordered taverns, and dining-houses – that, in order to compete with the attraction of these places, a mistress must be thoroughly acquainted with the theory and practice of cookery, as well as be perfectly conversant with all the other arts of making and keeping a comfortable home."

From *Mrs Beeton's Book of Household Management*

Isabella Beeton had married the much wealthier Samuel Beeton who was a publisher and instrumental in getting *Mrs Beeton's Book of Household Management* published. Not only was the book a manual on how to manage the home but it also included many recipes and information on the charitable duties that a mistress of the household was expected to perform. Unfortunately, Mrs Beeton's first child died in 1859 and then six years later she herself died from 'puerperal fever', aged only 28 years. Her book really helped many households at the time.

Engravings from *Mrs Beeton's Book of Household Management*

Advertising

Advertising became very important in Victorian times – there were so many new products that manufacturers had to work hard to sell their goods. The language used on the brightly coloured advertisements was very persuasive, to make people want to buy the goods.

Some advertisements were more informative than others.

BENHAM'S IMPROVED VENTILATING KITCHENER

It requires no Brickwork to fix it.
It Roasts, Bakes, Boils, and Steams with One Fire, and supplies a Bath if required.
It carries off the Heat and Smell of the Kitchen.
It can be fixed in its place in a few hours, after the Fireplace is cleared out and prepared for it, and by Local Workmen, if preferred.
It can be Removed, when required, in the event of a Change of Residence, being quite Detached and Independent.
It is not more expensive than the ordinary Kitcheners; whilst the cost of fixing is greatly diminished.

BENHAM & SONS,
50, 52, & 54, WIGMORE STREET, LONDON, W.

GRANT & Co., LONDON, MANCHESTER, & PARIS.

"Far too good to share"

Fry's CHOCOLATE
MAKERS TO H.M. THE KING.
300 GRANDS PRIX, GOLD MEDALS &c.

Victorian recipes

Ice cream and frozen delights

While some housekeepers prefer the old-fashioned freezer, many others use with very satisfactory results the **patent** freezer, the best of which we have ever seen is the White Mountain Freezer; it is durable, easily managed and greatly **expedites** the process of freezing.

To freeze cream quickly, have the ice pounded into small pieces, put a layer of ice and salt under the bottom of the freezer and back, and around the sides, cover the top of the tub with a blanket. When the cream hardens on the side of the freezer scrape down and beat it with a large iron spoon.

It is best to freeze ice cream in a warm place (the more rapid the melting of the ice the quicker the cream freezes), be watchful that no water or salt gets inside the freezer.

Ice cream may be formed into fanciful and ornamental shapes by using moulds made expressly for the purpose. After the cream is frozen put it in the moulds. Set in pounded ice and salt, cover close with a blanket until ready to serve.

Recipes

Vanilla ice cream
Dissolve half a teacup of arrowroot in a pint of milk, beat the whites of six eggs and the yolk of one and stir in, sweeten with loaf sugar, half a gallon of milk, set on the fire and let boil, then pour over the eggs and arrowroot. When cool pour in a quart of cream. Flavour with extract of vanilla; freeze.

Fruit ice cream
Half a gallon of new milk, one ounce of gelatine dissolved in cold milk and poured in, three eggs and four cups of sugar; pour in the freezer; as soon as it begins to freeze add a pound of raisins, one pint of strawberry preserves, one pound of chopped almonds, one grated cocoanut, one pound each of currants and citron; freeze.

Bisque
One gallon of rich custard, to which add two pounds of macaroons; freeze.

Toutes fruits ice cream
Take two quarts of rich cream, add one pound of pulverized sugar and four eggs, let come to a boil and stir until cool. Flavour with extract of vanilla; freeze and mix in thoroughly one pound in equal parts of preserved peaches, apricots, plums, cherries, pineapple, strawberries and quinces. Mix well with frozen cream.

From *Cookery and Housekeeping* by *A Veteran Housekeeper*, 1886

APPLE SNOW

INGREDIENTS:

METHOD:

The railway experience

Train travel was an amazing experience for Victorian travellers. They could move between towns more quickly than ever before. Some people were enthusiastic supporters of the railroads, but other people objected in the strongest terms.

Whatever one's opinion, however, it had to be admitted that railways changed the face of the country. As they spread through Britain, people moved away from the centres of cities, towards new areas called the suburbs. Wherever a station was built, houses soon followed.

For

I'm a railway navvy. I build the railway lines. The work is hard. We build viaducts, cuttings, tunnels and embankments by using our muscle power.

We suffer terribly from fumes and gas in the tunnels. There are many injuries. We work shifts round the clock and get no wages for any time off. But we are paid a good wage, about 30s. per week.

I am a manufacturer. I move all of my goods by rail now instead of the canals. The rate of carriage of goods is 10s. per ton; by canal it used to be 15s. per ton. My goods are delivered to their destination in two hours – and the same journey by barge took 20 hours! If I travel for business, it is cheaper by rail.

I am a charitable worker, trying to save the poor of the parish. I am in favour of the railways. Employment is found in the building and operation of the railways. Increased employment reduces the number of claimants for parochial relief. The railway pays one-fifth of the poor-rates in the parishes through which it passes. The railways also mean that fresh food and milk are carried cheaply to the cities.

Against

I am a shareholder in canals. The railways are making the countryside noisy and dangerous, with soot bellowing out across the land. When goods travelled by canal, the peace was not shattered by terrible mechanical trains. I have lost a great deal of money as people choose to travel and move goods by rail.

I am a coach driver. Before the establishment of the Liverpool and Manchester railway, there were 22 regular and about 7 occasional extra coaches between those places, which could only carry per day 688 persons. The railway carries 1,070 per day. All the coaches but one have ceased running, and that carries parcels.

I live in a house in Manchester due to be demolished by the railway company.

They are building the line through our kitchen! Houses are being knocked down, streets broken through and closed, deep water-filled pits and trenches are being dug in the ground, and enormous heaps of earth and clay are thrown up.

THE STAPLEHURST DISASTER

In 1865, Charles Dickens was travelling on the Folkestone Boat Express Train. He had been in Paris where he was resting before he was due to write his next novel, *Our Mutual Friend*. Unbeknown to him and the other 200 passengers, engineers had decided that essential repairs had to be done on the Beult Viaduct at Staplehurst in Kent.

The Folkestone Boat Train was a 'tidal' service, which only ran when the boats docked at Folkestone Harbour. The train on 9 June 1865 was due at the viaduct at 3pm, but the engineers had misread the timetable and had thought the train was due at 5pm. However, they did put out a warning flag before they started their repairs, then they removed the rails from the viaduct part of the track to allow them to work quickly.

Unfortunately, the train was travelling faster than the speed limit and although there was a warning flag the train could not stop in time before the gap in the track. Fortunately, Dickens was seated in the front carriage, which miraculously came to rest on the other side of the broken track, whereas the rest of the passenger carriages were left dangling over the side of the bridge, before dramatically plunging into the stream. Tragically, 10 passengers died and 49 were injured.

Would you prefer to travel in a first- or third-class train carriage? Why?

Third class:
- ❖ open wagons
- ❖ cushionless seats
- ❖ cold and wet in bad weather
- ❖ bare boards
- ❖ often overcrowded

First class
- ❖ closed carriages
- ❖ comfortable seating
- ❖ armrests
- ❖ fabric upholstery and decorations
- ❖ luggage space on roof

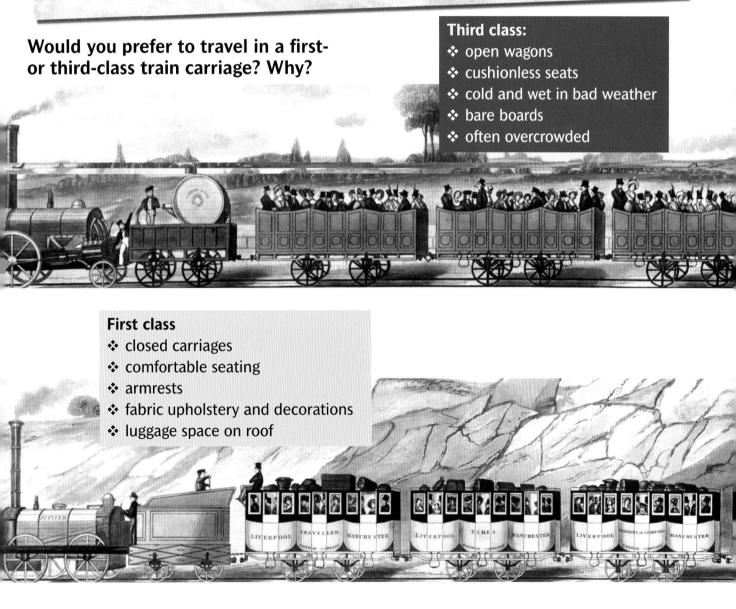

Railway developments

George Stephenson

George Stephenson (1781–1848) designed one of the first steam locomotives to successfully haul a load. He spent most of his working life designing and building railways and railway locomotives. He was helped by his son, Robert (1803–1859), who was also a successful railway builder and locomotive designer. Together, their work led to the building of railways throughout Britain.

How does a locomotive work?

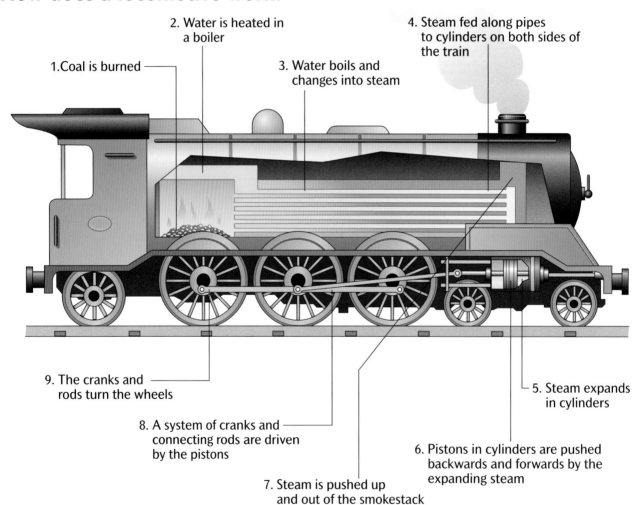

2. Water is heated in a boiler

4. Steam fed along pipes to cylinders on both sides of the train

1. Coal is burned

3. Water boils and changes into steam

9. The cranks and rods turn the wheels

5. Steam expands in cylinders

8. A system of cranks and connecting rods are driven by the pistons

6. Pistons in cylinders are pushed backwards and forwards by the expanding steam

7. Steam is pushed up and out of the smokestack

Did you know?

Before the railways there was no national standard time!

Victorian Railways timeline

. Great Western Railway express

Before electrification, the underground was run by steam.

Queen Victoria took her first trip on a train from Windsor to London

Railway mania (the rush to build railway lines) brought trains to the countryside

First four-mile stretch of London Underground opened between Paddington and Farringdon (run with steam power)

London Underground railway electrified (cleaner to use)

erpool–
nchester
way opened

| 330 | 1835-1841 | 1842 | 1844-1848 | 1851 | 1863 | 1871 | 1890s |

All main routes built

Brunel built the London to Bristol railway for the Great Western Railway company

Bank Holiday Act: certain days in the year became official holidays – the speed of trains meant coastal resorts such as Brighton and Blackpool could be developed

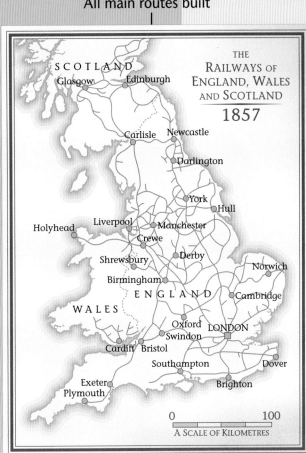

THE RAILWAYS OF ENGLAND, WALES AND SCOTLAND
1857

SCOTLAND
Glasgow   Edinburgh
Carlisle   Newcastle
Darlington
York   Hull
Liverpool   Manchester
Holyhead   Crewe
Shrewsbury   Derby
Birmingham   Norwich
ENGLAND   Cambridge
WALES
Oxford   LONDON
Cardiff   Swindon
Bristol
Southampton   Dover
Exeter   Brighton
Plymouth

0   100
A SCALE OF KILOMETRES

The railway network looked similar to today's.

Technological advances

Look at how new methods in coal mining helped to power engines which then helped to mine the coal.

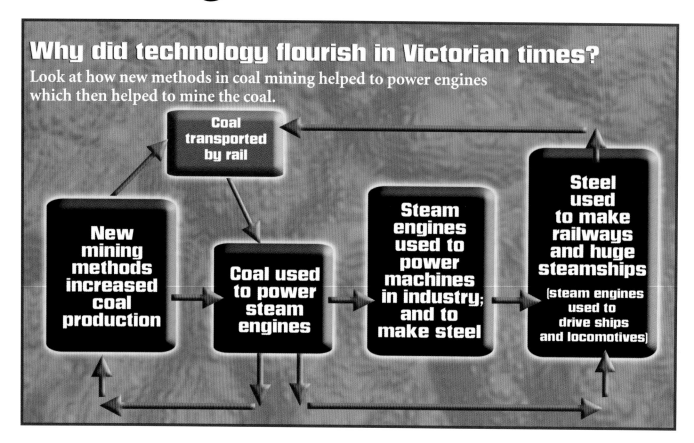

International communications

As the British **Empire** grew so did the need to communicate with the many **colonies** around the world. Letters would often take weeks before they reached their destinations, even when carried by the new steamships.

In 1937, the telegraph was invented and this helped to send messages faster across greater distances. The telegraph works by using electricity to send messages along wires. The messages were transmitted using Morse Code, invented by Samuel Morse in 1843. This was a system of dots and dashes tapped out at one end of the wire and then heard at the other end of the wire. The series of dots and dashes was a code, representing the different letters of the alphabet. The person receiving the telegraph message had to decipher the code into letters and words.

However, it wasn't until the first transatlantic telegraph cable was laid successfully between Britain and America in 1866 that the modern era of international communications really began.

Alexander Graham Bell was experimenting with a telegraph machine, sending more than one message at a time. As a result of his experiments, he began to work out how to transmit sounds and then developed the telephone. The telephone allowed people to actually speak to one another.

After the success of his invention, Bell also invented the **telephone exchange** as the demand for telephones increased. Telephone exchanges allowed several calls to happen at once. The first exchange in Britain was built in the 1870s but telephones did not become widespread until after the Victorian era.

How does a telephone work?

When a person speaks into a **telephone** their voice is changed by a microphone into electrical signals. These signals travel down a wire to another telephone. The signals are then changed back into sound waves by a loudspeaker in the telephone.

Cables from around the world were linked to landlines in this little telephone exchange in Porthcurno, Cornwall.

THE GREAT EXHIBITION

The exhibition's building became know as the 'Crystal Palace'. After the Great Exhibition closed, the Crystal Palace was moved to Sydenham Hill in South London.

On 1 May, 1851, Queen Victoria opened the Great Exhibition in Hyde Park in London. The building was enormous and contained over 13,000 exhibits. There were over 6,200,000 visitors to the exhibition.

Among the 13,000 exhibits from all around the world were an envelope machine, tools, kitchen appliances, steam locomotives, steel-making displays and even a model of the docks at Liverpool with 1600 fully rigged ships! The exhibition was a showcase for new technology, and showed that Britain was the 'Workshop of the World.'

Exhibit of industrial machinery

Leisure time

CYCLING

* Improvements to the roads
* 1873–1885 Penny-farthing was popular (speeds of up to 30 kph)
* 1885 Safety bicycles
* Women jeered for cycling – deemed indecent
* Women cyclists wore bloomers (invented 1849)

SEASIDE

* Thomas Cook promoted the idea of 'days out'
* Brighton and Blackpool developed as favourite seaside resorts
* Piers and promenades built
* 1860s fish and chip shops
* Invalids went to the seaside to improve their health

SPORTS

* 1872 Ist FA Cup final
* 1888 Football league set up
* Cricket (W.G. Grace 1848–1915: best British batsman)
* Tennis (1877: 1st Wimbledon championship)
* Horseracing very popular

LEISURE TIME

In early Victorian times, only rich people had 'leisure' time. Most poor people worked six days a week and had little money to do anything on a Sunday. In 1871, however, Bank Holidays were introduced and the 'railway day out' became popular.

PARKS

* Parks built as 'lungs' in cities for fresh-air walks
* Children taken for walks for their health
* Parks had formal flowerbeds and lawns

Restaurant and open-air dancing at Cremorne Gardens, London, 1858

The Empire

At its height, the British **Empire** covered more than one fifth of the surface of the world, and contained more than 370 million people. Other countries, such as France and Belgium, also had empires but Britain's was the largest. World maps, coloured to show who controlled different countries, were almost covered in pink – the colour of Britain's empire. Britain needed an empire to provide **raw materials** for **industry** and a market for the manufactured goods it produced.

The Empire was made up from countries all over the world, including Canada, Australia, New Zealand, South Africa and India. Queen Victoria was the Queen of all the countries that Britain controlled. Goods from the countries in the Empire were shipped to Britain, including tea, cloth, rubber and precious metals. Many people left Britain to work in 'The **Colonies**', with some creating little pockets of 'England' wherever they went, ignoring many of the wonderful things that made each country unique. The British were sure that they were the best people on Earth, and tried to change the lives of the people of the Empire. They even sent **missionaries** to 'civilize' the people of the Empire, often destroying the cultures and religions of those countries.

FOR

- Brought:
  - wealth
  - raw materials
  - precious metals
  - foods
- New plants and animals discovered
- Businesses created – Dutch East India Company
- Jobs for people in Britain and in the colonies
- Suez Canal built
- Missionaries – helped people

AGAINST

- Colonization:
  - native peoples forced to change to 'British' way of life as they were seen as barbaric and inferior
  - deaths of native peoples resisting colonization
- Stopped some trade between other countries, e.g. more tea from India rather than China
- Started own plantations in colonized countries (cheaper to trade)
- Missionaries – sometimes forced people to join a Christian religion
- Artificial country boundaries created – not taking into account the established tribal areas or kingdoms
- Wars in colonized countries (India and Africa)

In the 1890s, there was a major war between Britain and the **Boers** in South Africa.

Goods came from all around the world, including the Empire

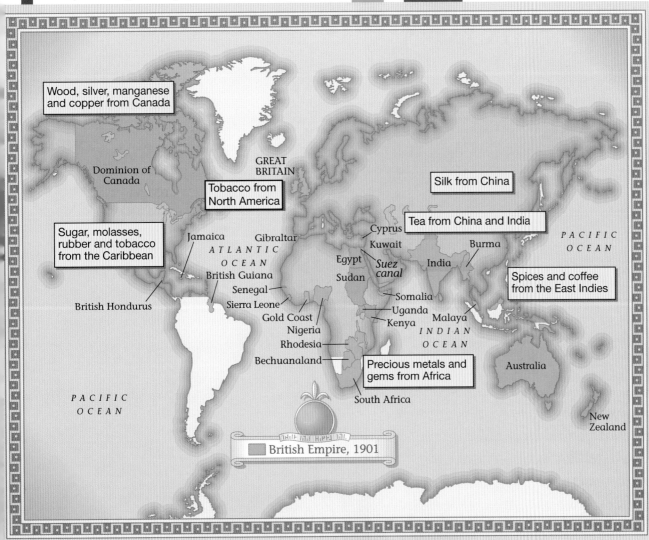

Wood, silver, manganese and copper from Canada

Dominion of Canada

GREAT BRITAIN

Tobacco from North America

Silk from China

Sugar, molasses, rubber and tobacco from the Caribbean

Jamaica

Gibraltar

ATLANTIC OCEAN

British Guiana

Senegal

Sierra Leone

Gold Coast

Nigeria

British Hondurus

Cyprus

Kuwait

Egypt

Sudan

Suez canal

Tea from China and India

Burma

India

PACIFIC OCEAN

Somalia

Uganda

Kenya

Malaya

Spices and coffee from the East Indies

Rhodesia

Bechuanaland

INDIAN OCEAN

Precious metals and gems from Africa

Australia

South Africa

PACIFIC OCEAN

New Zealand

British Empire, 1901

The Scramble for Africa

By 1880, the last continent not already added to an empire was Africa. Britain raced against other empire builders such as France and Belgium in what became known as the 'Scramble For Africa'. British soldiers took control of large parts of Africa, including Kenya, Egypt and Nigeria.

David Livingstone

Livingstone became a doctor and a missionary, and devoted much of his life to exploring Africa and to spreading the Christian gospel. He was one of the first Europeans to explore the central and southern parts of Africa. He decided that the best way to teach Africans about Christ was to travel around and see as many people as he could. This is how he became an explorer. In 1856, he travelled along the Zambezi River, and became the first European to see the spectacular Victoria Falls. He also became the first European to cross the entire width of southern Africa.

Victorian legacies

1889

Plaques tell us when buildings were constructed.

As you walk down the road, you can see things left behind by the Victorians everywhere! For example, there are great train stations, such as St Pancras in London, and museums, such as the Natural History Museum, also in London; in towns and villages across the country there are Victorian schools, houses, hospitals, churches, theatres – the Victorians were great builders!

Many houses are still standing that were built in Victorian times – not just big, grand houses but also terraces that housed railway workers, for example.

You may see Victorian 'street furniture' in places (for example, a red post box with the letters 'VR' standing for 'Victoria Regina' – Queen Victoria). In some places you can still see Victorian street lamps, adapted to take modern lighting.

Of course, we can also look at paintings, photographs and old books to learn about the Victorians.

Victoria and Albert Museum, London

An interesting place to look for evidence of Victorian life is a graveyard.

Epitaphs, the inscriptions carved into gravestones, are primary sources that give us valuable historical information. We can see that many women died in childbirth, because their death dates match the birth dates on the children's stones. Sadly, we can see that many children died very young, or even at birth.

SACRED
TO THE MEMORY OF
JOHN GOULD
SON OF JOHN AND JANE GOULD
WHO DIED JUNE 3rd 1854
AGED 3 YEARS
ALSO THOMAS EDWARD GOULD
SON OF THE ABOVE
WHO DIED FEB 12th 1864
AGED 3 YEARS & 9 MONTHS
FOR EVER WITH THE LORD
ALSO JANE GOULD DAUGHTER
OF THE ABOVE
WHO DIED SEPTR 20th 1868
AGED 6 YEARS

Viaducts and bridges

Industrial buildings

Victorian legacies

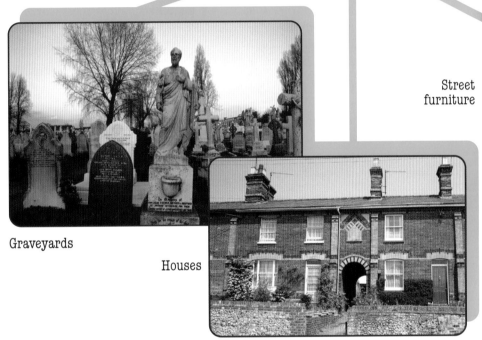
Graveyards

Houses

Street furniture

Then and Now

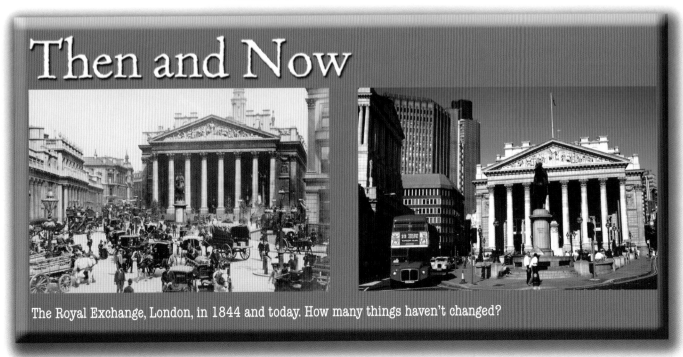
The Royal Exchange, London, in 1844 and today. How many things haven't changed?

Glossary

antiseptic A mixture spread over wounds to stop the growth of any germs that may cause diseases

Boers Dutch farmers who lived in South Africa

cesspit A hole for the disposal of waste including sewage

cholera A deadly disease caused by drinking dirty water

colonies The countries under British rule in the Victorian era

contaminated Containing poisons, such as sewage

copybooks Books that contained letters, words and sentences to copy

cutpurses Thieves and pickpockets who often roamed in gangs and slit the strings attaching purses to belts

empire A group of states or countries under the supreme rule of another country. The British Empire, shown on Victorian maps in pink, was very large

expedites Speeds up

home rule The right of a country to make its own decisions and laws

industry To do with trade (buying and selling things) or manufacturing (making things)

miasma A poisonous cloud of infection. The smell from the Thames, along with the infections the water carried, was often called a 'miasma'

middle class Businessmen and their families, together with professionals such as teachers, made up the new Victorian middle class

missionary Person from a religious community who travels around persuading people to take up their religion

modest Humble and not pure. Modest clothing hides much of the body

morals The principles of right and wrong behaviour

patent A patent grants the sole rights to make or sell an invention to a person or organization

pickpockets Criminals who stole things from people in the streets, for example by taking items from pockets, bags

phossy jaw A disease caused by the poisonous yellowish substance phosphorus ('phossy' is short for phosphorus). Phosphorous was used in the early match-making industry

raw materials Materials used to make products, for example wood is the raw material used to make paper

Reform Acts New laws made by Parliament

sanitation Making something clean and healthy

sewage Waste, for example from toilets and kitchens

sewers The pipes that take sewage away from houses

slums Overcrowded, dirty places to live, with poor facilities. A famous example is The Rookeries in Victorian London.

social reformers People who work on a campaign to make things better for others, e.g. Annie Besant and William Booth

sterilize To remove dangerous bacteria

suffragette A woman who wants women to have the right to vote

telephone exchange A place that links many telephone lines and services

tenements a set of apartments in one building

underclasses The poorest people in a society who had very little power, and who often suffered badly. They were the sort of people social reformers worked to help

upper class The aristocracy, including people with titles such as 'Lord' or 'Duchess'

workhouse A place run by the parish, where people could go to get food and somewhere to sleep in return for work. The food and conditions were poor and families were split up, so people lived in fear of going 'on the parish', or into the workhouse

working class People who worked in manufacturing (making things) or other industries, for wages

Bibliography

Non-fiction

The Vile Victorians (Horrible Histories), Terry Deary
ISBN: 0590554662

Who? What? When? Victorians, Bob Fowke
ISBN: 0340851848

Investigating the Victorians, Alison Honey
ISBN: 0707801672

The Victorians, Ann Kramer
ISBN: 0751357758

DK Eyewitness Guides: Victorians, Ann Kramer
ISBN: 0751364800

Victorians (The Past in Pictures), John Malam
ISBN: 0750226951

The Victorians (Craft Topics), R. Wright
ISBN: 0749641959

Fiction

A Christmas Carol, Charles Dickens, Illstr: Lisbeth Zwerger
ISBN: 0735812594

Smith, Leon Garfield
ISBN: 0374370826

Convict!, Julia Jarman
ISBN: 0749631295

The Sewer Sleuth, Julia Jarman
ISBN: 0749631287

The Lottie Project, Jaqueline Wilson
ISBN 0385407033

Websites

Channel 4 Learning
www.channel4.com/learning/microsites/Q/qca/victorians/

Learning Curve – based on photos and documents from the national Archive
http://learningcurve.pro.gov.uk/snapshots/snapshot05/snapshot5.htm - How did the victorians have fun?
http://learningcurve.pro.gov.uk/snapshots/snapshot14/snapshot14.htm - Comparing homes of the rich and poor

BBC Visit a Victorian street
www.bbc.co.uk/history/walk/games_index.shtml

Spartacus Online Encyclopaedia
www.spartacus.schoolnet.co.uk/IRchild.main.htm

Places to visit

Beamish Open Air Museum
http://www.beamish.org.uk/
'… no ordinary museum but a living, working experience of life as it was in the Great North in the early 1800s and 1900s.'

Blists Hill Victorian Town (Open Air Museum)
Madeley, Telford, Shropshire TF8 7EF
Tel: 01952 433522
http://www.ironbridge.org.uk/v_blists.asp
A small Victorian town has been created above 30 acres of woodland walks on the banks of the Shropshire Canal.

Ragged School Museum
46-50 Copperfield Road, London E3 4RR
Tel: 020 8980 6405
http://www.raggedschoolmuseum.org.uk/index.html

Florence Nightingale Museum
2 Lambeth Palace Road, London SE1 7EW
Tel: (0044) 171 620 0374
http://www.florence-nightingale.co.uk/

National Museum of Childhood
Bethnal Green, Cambridge Heath Road, London E2 9PA
Tel: 020 8983 5200
http://www.vam.ac.uk/vastatic/nmc/index.html

British Engineering Museum of Steam and Mechanical Antiquities
off Nevill Road, Hove, Sussex BN3 7QA
Tel: 01273 559583
Restored Victorian pumping station; also traction engines and fire engines, plus an interactive exhibition for children. Boilers are fired up each month and on bank holidays

Preston Hall Museum
Yarm Road, Stockton-on-Tees TS18 3RH
Tel: 01642 781184
www.train.stockton.gov.uk
Preston Hall features a Victorian street you can walk through, set in around 1900

Index